YOUR STORY

I have known _____ since I w
  PARTNER 1

old. The best way to describe _____ is that they are
                                PARTNER 1

a/an _____ _____ . My _____
      ADJECTIVE   NOUN   ADJECTIVE

memory with _____ happened in _____ .
              PARTNER 1   YEAR

We were at _____ with _____ .
             PLACE   PERSON/PEOPLE

It was _____ because _____ .
        ADJECTIVE

When _____ first introduced me to _____ ,
       PARTNER 1   PARTNER 2

I thought, _____ ! My _____
              EXCLAMATION   ADJECTIVE

memory of the couple is _____ .

They make the _____ couple because
                 ADJECTIVE

_____ .

_____ is _____ .
  PARTNER 1   ADJECTIVE

_____ is _____ .
  PARTNER 2   ADJECTIVE

Together they are _____ .
                     ADJECTIVE

All my _____ ,
          NOUN

_____
         NAME

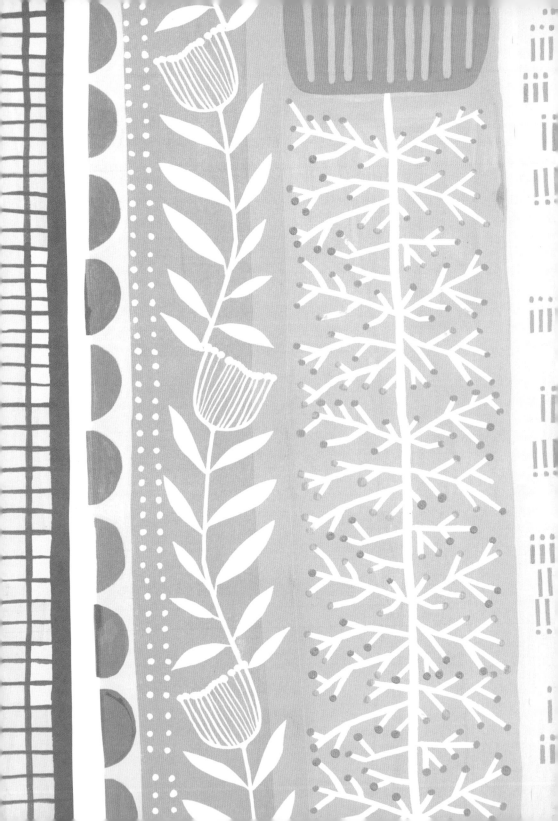

WISHES & ADVICE

The _____ ingredient to a/an _____
        ADJECTIVE   ADJECTIVE

marriage is _____ . In the _____ year,
              NOUN   LOW NUMBER

you should _____ . In the _____ year,
                                        HIGH NUMBER

you should _____ .

Always _____ . Never _____ .

Occasionally _____ .

You will argue about _____ . It doesn't matter
                        NOUN

because _____ .

My advice in a haiku:

_____
        5 SYLLABLES

_____
        7 SYLLABLES

_____
        5 SYLLABLES

Most of all, I wish you _____ .
                            NOUN

With _____ ,
        NOUN

_____
        NAME

ADVENTURES TO SHARE

If the couple was a destination, they would be _____
                                                    PLACE

because _____ . On your honeymoon, be sure

to _____ _____ . Don't _____
      VERB   NOUN   VERB

_____ . The most _____ trip I've taken was
      NOUN   ADJECTIVE

to _____ . The _____ thing I've eaten on
      PLACE   ADJECTIVE

vacation was _____ in _____ . One activity
                  FOOD   PLACE

the couple should try is _____ in _____ .
                          VERB ENDING IN "ING"   PLACE

A mini-adventure the couple should have together is

_____ .

Top three to-dos for the couple's bucket list:

1. _____ 2. _____ 3. _____

Draw the couple a picture of your favorite destination:

Wishing you _____ adventures together,
                ADJECTIVE

_____
              NAME

YOUR STORY

I have known _____ since I was _____ years
PARTNER 1 NUMBER

old. The best way to describe _____ is that they are
PARTNER 1

a/an _____ _____ . My _____
ADJECTIVE NOUN ADJECTIVE

memory with _____ happened in _____ .
PARTNER 1 YEAR

We were at _____ with _____ .
PLACE PERSON/PEOPLE

It was _____ because _____ .
ADJECTIVE

When _____ first introduced me to _____ ,
PARTNER 1 PARTNER 2

I thought, _____ ! My _____
EXCLAMATION ADJECTIVE

memory of the couple is _____ .

They make the _____ couple because
ADJECTIVE

_____ .

_____ is _____ .
PARTNER 1 ADJECTIVE

_____ is _____ .
PARTNER 2 ADJECTIVE

Together they are _____ .
ADJECTIVE

All my _____ ,
NOUN

_____
NAME

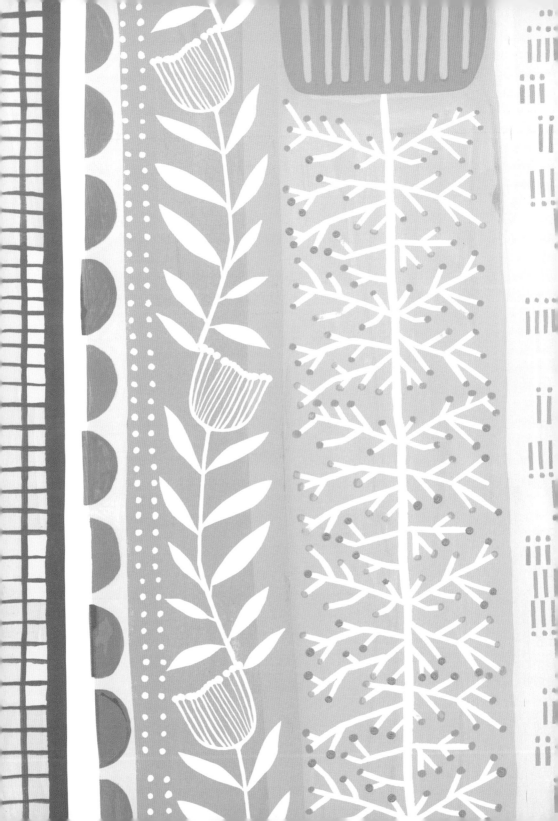

WISHES & ADVICE

The _____ ingredient to a/an _____
        ADJECTIVE   ADJECTIVE

marriage is _____ . In the _____ year,
                  NOUN   LOW NUMBER

you should _____ . In the _____ year,
                                          HIGH NUMBER

you should _____ .

Always _____ . Never _____ .

Occasionally _____ .

You will argue about _____ . It doesn't matter
                           NOUN

because _____ .

My advice in a haiku:

_____
              5 SYLLABLES

_____
              7 SYLLABLES

_____
              5 SYLLABLES

Most of all, I wish you _____ .
                               NOUN

With _____ ,
          NOUN

_____
              NAME

ADVENTURES TO SHARE

If the couple was a destination, they would be _____
PLACE

because _____ . On your honeymoon, be sure

to _____ _____ . Don't _____
VERB   NOUN   VERB

_____ . The most _____ trip I've taken was
NOUN   ADJECTIVE

to _____ . The _____ thing I've eaten on
PLACE   ADJECTIVE

vacation was _____ in _____ . One activity
FOOD   PLACE

the couple should try is _____ in _____ .
VERB ENDING IN "ING"   PLACE

A mini-adventure the couple should have together is

_____ .

Top three to-dos for the couple's bucket list:

1. _____ 2. _____ 3. _____

Draw the couple a picture of your favorite destination:

Wishing you _____ adventures together,
ADJECTIVE

_____
NAME

YOUR STORY

I have known _____ since I was _____ years
              PARTNER 1   NUMBER

old. The best way to describe _____ is that they are
                                  PARTNER 1

a/an _____ _____ . My _____
         ADJECTIVE   NOUN   ADJECTIVE

memory with _____ happened in _____ .
                PARTNER 1   YEAR

We were at _____ with _____ .
               PLACE   PERSON/PEOPLE

It was _____ because _____ .
          ADJECTIVE

When _____ first introduced me to _____ ,
         PARTNER 1   PARTNER 2

I thought, _____ ! My _____
              EXCLAMATION   ADJECTIVE

memory of the couple is _____ .

They make the _____ couple because
                  ADJECTIVE

_____ .

_____ is _____ .
    PARTNER 1   ADJECTIVE

_____ is _____ .
    PARTNER 2   ADJECTIVE

Together they are _____ .
                      ADJECTIVE

All my _____ ,
          NOUN

_____
      NAME

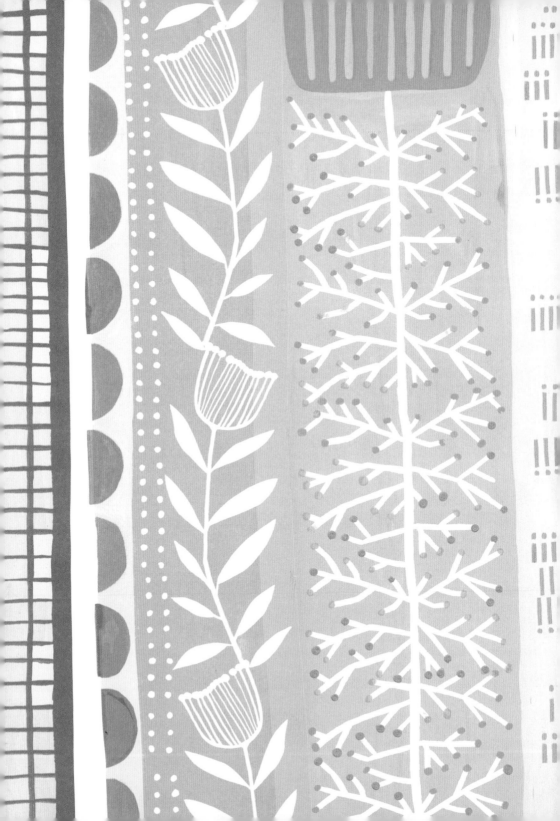

WISHES & ADVICE

The _____ ingredient to a/an _____
        ADJECTIVE   ADJECTIVE

marriage is _____ . In the _____ year,
              NOUN   LOW NUMBER

you should _____ . In the _____ year,
                                 HIGH NUMBER

you should _____ .

Always _____ . Never _____ .

Occasionally _____ .

You will argue about _____ . It doesn't matter
                           NOUN

because _____ .

My advice in a haiku:

_____
5 SYLLABLES

_____
7 SYLLABLES

_____
5 SYLLABLES

Most of all, I wish you _____ .
                               NOUN

With _____ ,
           NOUN

_____
NAME

ADVENTURES TO SHARE

If the couple was a destination, they would be _____
                                                   PLACE

because _____ . On your honeymoon, be sure

to _____ _____ . Don't _____
      VERB   NOUN   VERB

_____ . The most _____ trip I've taken was
      NOUN   ADJECTIVE

to _____ . The _____ thing I've eaten on
      PLACE   ADJECTIVE

vacation was _____ in _____ . One activity
                  FOOD   PLACE

the couple should try is _____ in _____ .
                         VERB ENDING IN "ING"   PLACE

A mini-adventure the couple should have together is

_____ .

Top three to-dos for the couple's bucket list:

1. _____ 2. _____ 3. _____

Draw the couple a picture of your favorite destination:

Wishing you _____ adventures together,
                ADJECTIVE

_____
              NAME

YOUR STORY

I have known _____ since I was _____ years
PARTNER 1   NUMBER

old. The best way to describe _____ is that they are
                              PARTNER 1

a/an _____ _____. My _____
      ADJECTIVE   NOUN   ADJECTIVE

memory with _____ happened in _____.
              PARTNER 1   YEAR

We were at _____ with _____.
              PLACE   PERSON/PEOPLE

It was _____ because _____.
         ADJECTIVE

When _____ first introduced me to _____,
       PARTNER 1   PARTNER 2

I thought, _____! My _____
            EXCLAMATION   ADJECTIVE

memory of the couple is _____.

They make the _____ couple because
                ADJECTIVE

_____.

_____ is _____.
PARTNER 1   ADJECTIVE

_____ is _____.
PARTNER 2   ADJECTIVE

Together they are _____.
                    ADJECTIVE

All my _____,
         NOUN

_____
NAME

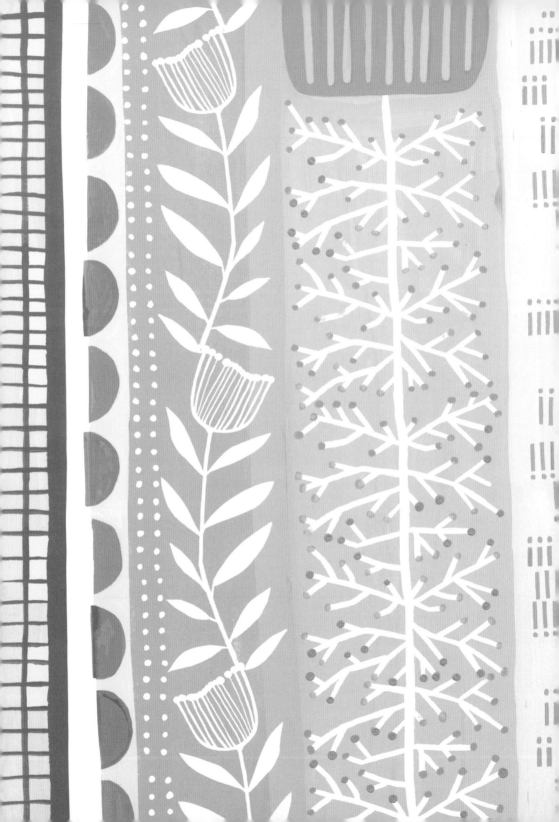

WISHES & ADVICE

The _____ ingredient to a/an _____
    ADJECTIVE   ADJECTIVE

marriage is _____ . In the _____ year,
      NOUN   LOW NUMBER

you should _____ . In the _____ year,
              HIGH NUMBER

you should _____ .

Always _____ . Never _____ .

Occasionally _____ .

You will argue about _____ . It doesn't matter
          NOUN

because _____ .

My advice in a haiku:

_____
5 SYLLABLES

_____
7 SYLLABLES

_____
5 SYLLABLES

Most of all, I wish you _____ .
            NOUN

With _____ ,
     NOUN

_____
NAME

ADVENTURES TO SHARE

If the couple was a destination, they would be _____
PLACE

because _____ . On your honeymoon, be sure

to _____ _____ . Don't _____
VERB   NOUN   VERB

_____ . The most _____ trip I've taken was
NOUN   ADJECTIVE

to _____ . The _____ thing I've eaten on
PLACE   ADJECTIVE

vacation was _____ in _____ . One activity
FOOD   PLACE

the couple should try is _____ in _____ .
VERB ENDING IN "ING"   PLACE

A mini-adventure the couple should have together is

_____ .

Top three to-dos for the couple's bucket list:

1. _____   2. _____   3. _____

Draw the couple a picture of your favorite destination:

Wishing you _____ adventures together,
ADJECTIVE

_____
NAME

YOUR STORY

I have known _____ since I was _____ years
　　　　　　　　PARTNER 1　　　　　　　　　　　　NUMBER

old. The best way to describe _____ is that they are
　　　　　　　　　　　　　　　　　PARTNER 1

a/an _____ _____ . My _____
　　　　　ADJECTIVE　　　　　　NOUN　　　　　　　　ADJECTIVE

memory with _____ happened in _____ .
　　　　　　　　PARTNER 1　　　　　　　　　　　YEAR

We were at _____ with _____ .
　　　　　　　　　PLACE　　　　　　　　PERSON/PEOPLE

It was _____ because _____ .
　　　　ADJECTIVE

When _____ first introduced me to _____ ,
　　　　PARTNER 1　　　　　　　　　　　　　　　PARTNER 2

I thought, _____ ! My _____
　　　　　　　EXCLAMATION　　　　　　　　ADJECTIVE

memory of the couple is _____ .

They make the _____ couple because
　　　　　　　　　ADJECTIVE

_____ .

_____ is _____ .
PARTNER 1　　　　　　　　　ADJECTIVE

_____ is _____ .
PARTNER 2　　　　　　　　　ADJECTIVE

Together they are _____ .
　　　　　　　　　　　ADJECTIVE

All my _____ ,
　　　　　　NOUN

_____
NAME

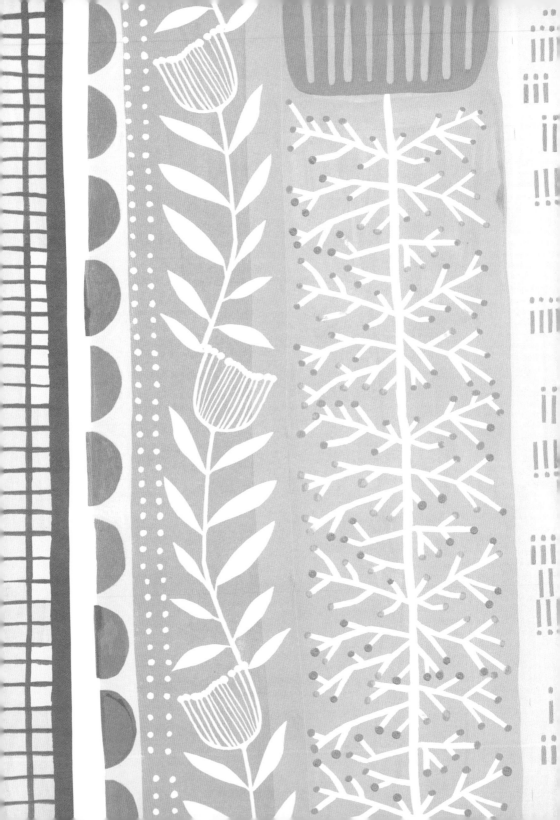

WISHES & ADVICE

The _____ ingredient to a/an _____
      ADJECTIVE   ADJECTIVE

marriage is _____ . In the _____ year,
                  NOUN   LOW NUMBER

you should _____ . In the _____ year,
                                          HIGH NUMBER

you should _____ .

Always _____ . Never _____ .

Occasionally _____ .

You will argue about _____ . It doesn't matter
                          NOUN

because _____ .

My advice in a haiku:

_____
5 SYLLABLES

_____
7 SYLLABLES

_____
5 SYLLABLES

Most of all, I wish you _____ .
                              NOUN

With _____ ,
          NOUN

_____
NAME

ADVENTURES TO SHARE

If the couple was a destination, they would be _____
PLACE

because _____ . On your honeymoon, be sure

to _____ _____ . Don't _____
VERB   NOUN   VERB

_____ . The most _____ trip I've taken was
NOUN   ADJECTIVE

to _____ . The _____ thing I've eaten on
PLACE   ADJECTIVE

vacation was _____ in _____ . One activity
FOOD   PLACE

the couple should try is _____ in _____ .
VERB ENDING IN "ING"   PLACE

A mini-adventure the couple should have together is

_____ .

Top three to-dos for the couple's bucket list:

1. _____ 2. _____ 3. _____

Draw the couple a picture of your favorite destination:

Wishing you _____ adventures together,
ADJECTIVE

_____
NAME

YOUR STORY

I have known _____ since I was _____ years
PARTNER 1   NUMBER

old. The best way to describe _____ is that they are
PARTNER 1

a/an _____ _____ . My _____
ADJECTIVE   NOUN   ADJECTIVE

memory with _____ happened in _____ .
PARTNER 1   YEAR

We were at _____ with _____ .
PLACE   PERSON/PEOPLE

It was _____ because _____ .
ADJECTIVE

When _____ first introduced me to _____ ,
PARTNER 1   PARTNER 2

I thought, _____ ! My _____
EXCLAMATION   ADJECTIVE

memory of the couple is _____ .

They make the _____ couple because
ADJECTIVE

_____ .

_____ is _____ .
PARTNER 1   ADJECTIVE

_____ is _____ .
PARTNER 2   ADJECTIVE

Together they are _____ .
ADJECTIVE

All my _____ ,
NOUN

_____
NAME

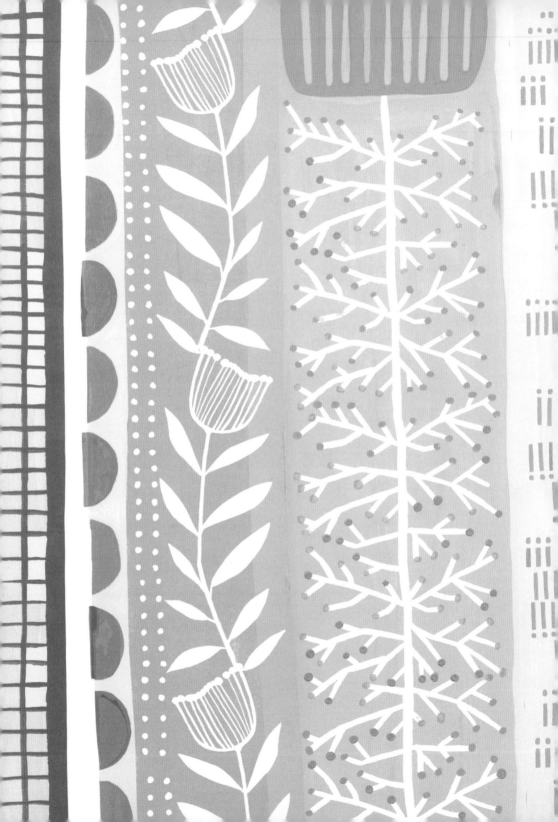

WISHES & ADVICE

The _____ ingredient to a/an _____
       ADJECTIVE   ADJECTIVE

marriage is _____ . In the _____ year,
             NOUN   LOW NUMBER

you should _____ . In the _____ year,
                                 HIGH NUMBER

you should _____ .

Always _____ . Never _____ .

Occasionally _____ .

You will argue about _____ . It doesn't matter
                      NOUN

because _____ .

My advice in a haiku:

_____
5 SYLLABLES

_____
7 SYLLABLES

_____
5 SYLLABLES

Most of all, I wish you _____ .
                              NOUN

With _____ ,
            NOUN

_____
NAME

ADVENTURES TO SHARE

If the couple was a destination, they would be _____
PLACE

because _____ . On your honeymoon, be sure

to _____ _____ . Don't _____
VERB   NOUN   VERB

_____ . The most _____ trip I've taken was
NOUN   ADJECTIVE

to _____ . The _____ thing I've eaten on
PLACE   ADJECTIVE

vacation was _____ in _____ . One activity
FOOD   PLACE

the couple should try is _____ in _____ .
VERB ENDING IN "ING"   PLACE

A mini-adventure the couple should have together is

_____ .

Top three to-dos for the couple's bucket list:

1. _____ 2. _____ 3. _____

Draw the couple a picture of your favorite destination:

Wishing you _____ adventures together,
ADJECTIVE

_____
NAME

YOUR STORY

I have known _____ since I was _____ years
                  PARTNER 1   NUMBER

old. The best way to describe _____ is that they are
                                    PARTNER 1

a/an _____ _____ . My _____
          ADJECTIVE   NOUN   ADJECTIVE

memory with _____ happened in _____ .
                 PARTNER 1   YEAR

We were at _____ with _____ .
                  PLACE   PERSON/PEOPLE

It was _____ because _____ .
          ADJECTIVE

When _____ first introduced me to _____ ,
          PARTNER 1   PARTNER 2

I thought, _____ ! My _____
              EXCLAMATION   ADJECTIVE

memory of the couple is _____ .

They make the _____ couple because
                   ADJECTIVE

_____ .

_____ is _____ .
   PARTNER 1   ADJECTIVE

_____ is _____ .
   PARTNER 2   ADJECTIVE

Together they are _____ .
                        ADJECTIVE

All my _____ ,
            NOUN

_____
       NAME

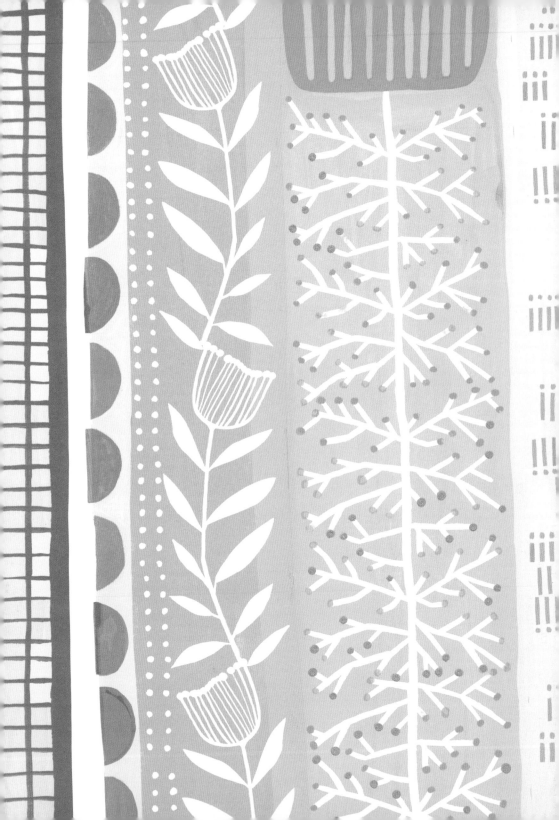

WISHES & ADVICE

The _____ ingredient to a/an _____
          ADJECTIVE   ADJECTIVE

marriage is _____ . In the _____ year,
                  NOUN   LOW NUMBER

you should _____ . In the _____ year,
                                          HIGH NUMBER

you should _____ .

Always _____ . Never _____ .

Occasionally _____ .

You will argue about _____ . It doesn't matter
                            NOUN

because _____ .

My advice in a haiku:

_____
          5 SYLLABLES

_____
          7 SYLLABLES

_____
          5 SYLLABLES

Most of all, I wish you _____ .
                              NOUN

With _____ ,
          NOUN

_____
          NAME

ADVENTURES TO SHARE

If the couple was a destination, they would be _____
PLACE

because _____ . On your honeymoon, be sure

to _____ _____ . Don't _____
VERB   NOUN   VERB

_____ . The most _____ trip I've taken was
NOUN   ADJECTIVE

to _____ . The _____ thing I've eaten on
PLACE   ADJECTIVE

vacation was _____ in _____ . One activity
FOOD   PLACE

the couple should try is _____ in _____ .
VERB ENDING IN "ING"   PLACE

A mini-adventure the couple should have together is

_____ .

Top three to-dos for the couple's bucket list:

1. _____ 2. _____ 3. _____

Draw the couple a picture of your favorite destination:

Wishing you _____ adventures together,
ADJECTIVE

_____
NAME

YOUR STORY

I have known _____ since I was _____ years
 PARTNER 1   NUMBER

old. The best way to describe _____ is that they are
                                      PARTNER 1

a/an _____ _____ . My _____
        ADJECTIVE   NOUN   ADJECTIVE

memory with _____ happened in _____ .
                   PARTNER 1   YEAR

We were at _____ with _____ .
                 PLACE   PERSON/PEOPLE

It was _____ because _____ .
          ADJECTIVE

When _____ first introduced me to _____ ,
          PARTNER 1   PARTNER 2

I thought, _____ ! My _____
                EXCLAMATION   ADJECTIVE

memory of the couple is _____ .

They make the _____ couple because
                   ADJECTIVE

_____ .

_____ is _____ .
      PARTNER 1   ADJECTIVE

_____ is _____ .
      PARTNER 2   ADJECTIVE

Together they are _____ .
                        ADJECTIVE

All my _____ ,
            NOUN

_____
      NAME

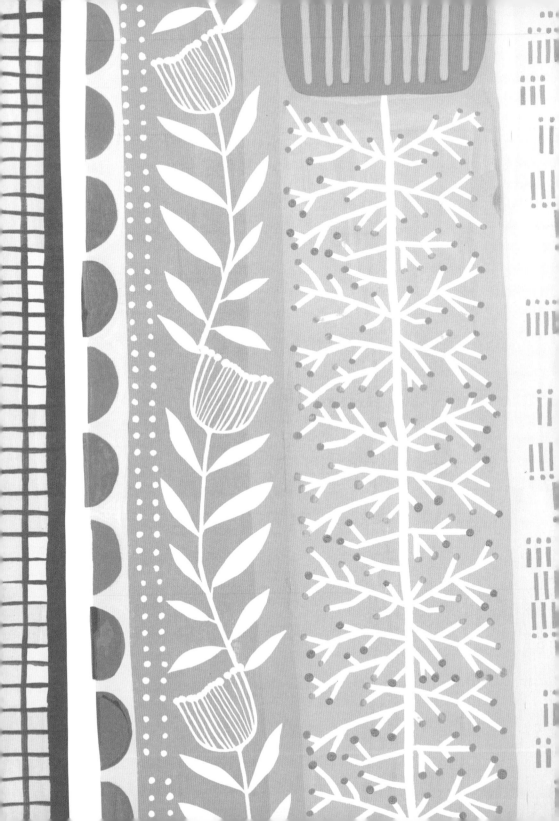

WISHES & ADVICE

The _____ ingredient to a/an _____
        ADJECTIVE   ADJECTIVE

marriage is _____ . In the _____ year,
                NOUN   LOW NUMBER

you should _____ . In the _____ year,
                                        HIGH NUMBER

you should _____ .

Always _____ . Never _____ .

Occasionally _____ .

You will argue about _____ . It doesn't matter
                            NOUN

because _____ .

My advice in a haiku:

_____
        5 SYLLABLES

_____
        7 SYLLABLES

_____
        5 SYLLABLES

Most of all, I wish you _____ .
                                NOUN

With _____ ,
            NOUN

_____
        NAME

ADVENTURES TO SHARE

If the couple was a destination, they would be _____
PLACE

because _____ . On your honeymoon, be sure

to _____ _____ . Don't _____
VERB   NOUN   VERB

_____ . The most _____ trip I've taken was
NOUN   ADJECTIVE

to _____ . The _____ thing I've eaten on
PLACE   ADJECTIVE

vacation was _____ in _____ . One activity
FOOD   PLACE

the couple should try is _____ in _____ .
VERB ENDING IN "ING"   PLACE

A mini-adventure the couple should have together is

_____ .

Top three to-dos for the couple's bucket list:

1. _____ 2. _____ 3. _____

Draw the couple a picture of your favorite destination:

Wishing you _____ adventures together,
ADJECTIVE

_____
NAME

YOUR STORY

I have known _____ since I was _____ years
PARTNER 1 NUMBER

old. The best way to describe _____ is that they are
PARTNER 1

a/an _____ _____ . My _____
ADJECTIVE NOUN ADJECTIVE

memory with _____ happened in _____ .
PARTNER 1 YEAR

We were at _____ with _____ .
PLACE PERSON/PEOPLE

It was _____ because _____ .
ADJECTIVE

When _____ first introduced me to _____ ,
PARTNER 1 PARTNER 2

I thought, _____ ! My _____
EXCLAMATION ADJECTIVE

memory of the couple is _____ .

They make the _____ couple because
ADJECTIVE

_____ .

_____ is _____ .
PARTNER 1 ADJECTIVE

_____ is _____ .
PARTNER 2 ADJECTIVE

Together they are _____ .
ADJECTIVE

All my _____ ,
NOUN

_____
NAME

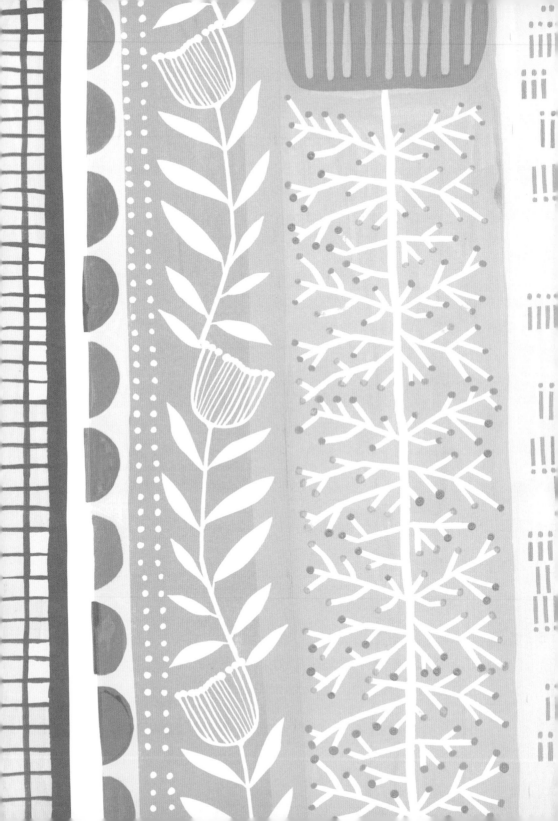

WISHES & ADVICE

The _____ ingredient to a/an _____
        ADJECTIVE   ADJECTIVE

marriage is _____ . In the _____ year,
                   NOUN   LOW NUMBER

you should _____ . In the _____ year,
                                          HIGH NUMBER

you should _____ .

Always _____ . Never _____ .

Occasionally _____ .

You will argue about _____ . It doesn't matter
                              NOUN

because _____ .

My advice in a haiku:

_____
              5 SYLLABLES

_____
              7 SYLLABLES

_____
              5 SYLLABLES

Most of all, I wish you _____ .
                                   NOUN

With _____ ,
            NOUN

_____
              NAME

ADVENTURES TO SHARE

If the couple was a destination, they would be _____
PLACE

because _____ . On your honeymoon, be sure

to _____ _____ . Don't _____
VERB   NOUN   VERB

_____ . The most _____ trip I've taken was
NOUN   ADJECTIVE

to _____ . The _____ thing I've eaten on
PLACE   ADJECTIVE

vacation was _____ in _____ . One activity
FOOD   PLACE

the couple should try is _____ in _____ .
VERB ENDING IN "ING"   PLACE

A mini-adventure the couple should have together is

_____ .

Top three to-dos for the couple's bucket list:

1. _____   2. _____   3. _____

Draw the couple a picture of your favorite destination:

Wishing you _____ adventures together,
ADJECTIVE

_____
NAME

YOUR STORY

I have known _____ since I was _____ years
_{PARTNER 1}   _{NUMBER}

old. The best way to describe _____ is that they are
_{PARTNER 1}

a/an _____ _____ . My _____
_{ADJECTIVE}   _{NOUN}   _{ADJECTIVE}

memory with _____ happened in _____ .
_{PARTNER 1}   _{YEAR}

We were at _____ with _____ .
_{PLACE}   _{PERSON/PEOPLE}

It was _____ because _____ .
_{ADJECTIVE}

When _____ first introduced me to _____ ,
_{PARTNER 1}   _{PARTNER 2}

I thought, _____ ! My _____
_{EXCLAMATION}   _{ADJECTIVE}

memory of the couple is _____ .

They make the _____ couple because
_{ADJECTIVE}

_____ .

_____ is _____ .
_{PARTNER 1}   _{ADJECTIVE}

_____ is _____ .
_{PARTNER 2}   _{ADJECTIVE}

Together they are _____ .
_{ADJECTIVE}

All my _____ ,
_{NOUN}

_____
_{NAME}

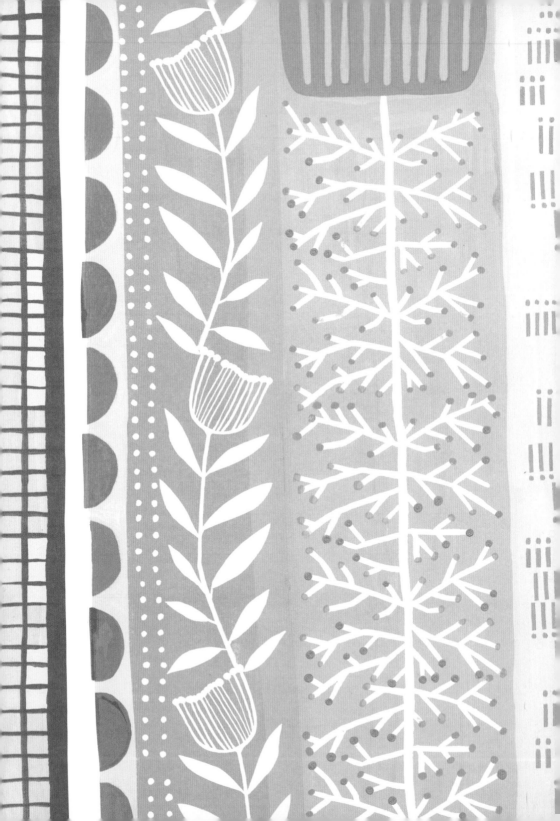

WISHES & ADVICE

The _____ ingredient to a/an _____
     ADJECTIVE   ADJECTIVE

marriage is _____ . In the _____ year,
              NOUN   LOW NUMBER

you should _____ . In the _____ year,
                                 HIGH NUMBER

      you should _____ .

Always _____ . Never _____ .

      Occasionally _____ .

You will argue about _____ . It doesn't matter
                      NOUN

because _____ .

      My advice in a haiku:

_____
            5 SYLLABLES

_____
            7 SYLLABLES

_____
            5 SYLLABLES

Most of all, I wish you _____ .
                         NOUN

With _____ ,
          NOUN

_____
            NAME

ADVENTURES TO SHARE

If the couple was a destination, they would be _____
PLACE

because _____ . On your honeymoon, be sure

to _____ _____ . Don't _____
VERB NOUN VERB

_____ . The most _____ trip I've taken was
NOUN ADJECTIVE

to _____ . The _____ thing I've eaten on
PLACE ADJECTIVE

vacation was _____ in _____ . One activity
FOOD PLACE

the couple should try is _____ in _____ .
VERB ENDING IN "ING" PLACE

A mini-adventure the couple should have together is

_____ .

Top three to-dos for the couple's bucket list:

1. _____ 2. _____ 3. _____

Draw the couple a picture of your favorite destination:

Wishing you _____ adventures together,
ADJECTIVE

_____
NAME

YOUR STORY

I have known _____ since I was _____ years
PARTNER 1 / NUMBER

old. The best way to describe _____ is that they are
PARTNER 1

a/an _____ _____ . My _____
ADJECTIVE / NOUN / ADJECTIVE

memory with _____ happened in _____ .
PARTNER 1 / YEAR

We were at _____ with _____ .
PLACE / PERSON/PEOPLE

It was _____ because _____ .
ADJECTIVE

When _____ first introduced me to _____ ,
PARTNER 1 / PARTNER 2

I thought, _____ ! My _____
EXCLAMATION / ADJECTIVE

memory of the couple is _____ .

They make the _____ couple because
ADJECTIVE

_____ .

_____ is _____ .
PARTNER 1 / ADJECTIVE

_____ is _____ .
PARTNER 2 / ADJECTIVE

Together they are _____ .
ADJECTIVE

All my _____ ,
NOUN

_____
NAME

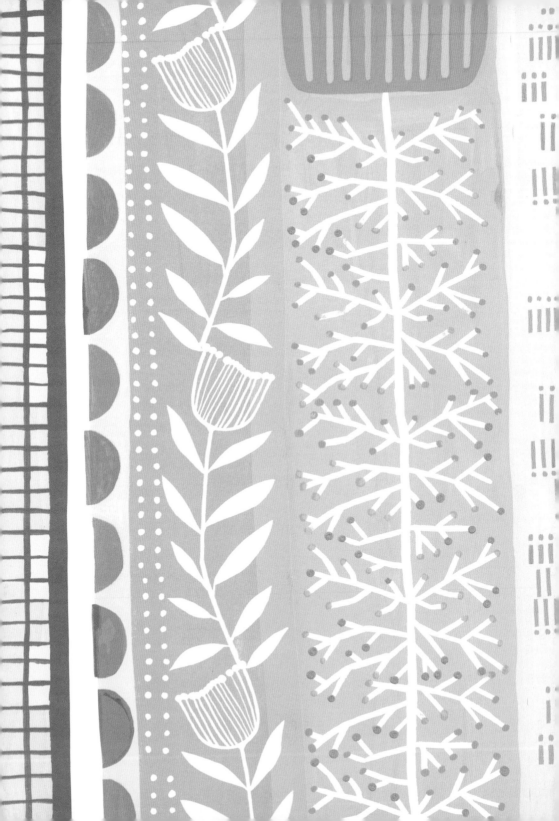

WISHES & ADVICE

The _____ ingredient to a/an _____
ADJECTIVE   ADJECTIVE

marriage is _____ . In the _____ year,
NOUN   LOW NUMBER

you should _____ . In the _____ year,
                                        HIGH NUMBER

you should _____ .

Always _____ . Never _____ .

Occasionally _____ .

You will argue about _____ . It doesn't matter
NOUN

because _____ .

My advice in a haiku:

_____
5 SYLLABLES

_____
7 SYLLABLES

_____
5 SYLLABLES

Most of all, I wish you _____ .
NOUN

With _____ ,
NOUN

_____
NAME

ADVENTURES TO SHARE

If the couple was a destination, they would be _____
PLACE

because _____ . On your honeymoon, be sure

to _____ _____ . Don't _____
VERB   NOUN   VERB

_____ . The most _____ trip I've taken was
NOUN   ADJECTIVE

to _____ . The _____ thing I've eaten on
PLACE   ADJECTIVE

vacation was _____ in _____ . One activity
FOOD   PLACE

the couple should try is _____ in _____ .
VERB ENDING IN "ING"   PLACE

A mini-adventure the couple should have together is

_____ .

Top three to-dos for the couple's bucket list:

1. _____ 2. _____ 3. _____

Draw the couple a picture of your favorite destination:

Wishing you _____ adventures together,
ADJECTIVE

_____
NAME

YOUR STORY

I have known _____ since I was _____ years
　　　　　　　　　PARTNER 1　　　　　　　　　　　NUMBER

old. The best way to describe _____ is that they are
　　　　　　　　　　　　　　　　　　PARTNER 1

a/an _____ _____ . My _____
　　　　ADJECTIVE　　　　　　　NOUN　　　　　　　　　　ADJECTIVE

memory with _____ happened in _____ .
　　　　　　　　PARTNER 1　　　　　　　　　　　　　YEAR

We were at _____ with _____ .
　　　　　　　　PLACE　　　　　　　　　PERSON/PEOPLE

It was _____ because _____ .
　　　　　ADJECTIVE

When _____ first introduced me to _____ ,
　　　　　PARTNER 1　　　　　　　　　　　　　　　　PARTNER 2

I thought, _____ ! My _____
　　　　　　　EXCLAMATION　　　　　　　　　ADJECTIVE

memory of the couple is _____ .

They make the _____ couple because
　　　　　　　　　ADJECTIVE

_____ .

_____ is _____ .
　　PARTNER 1　　　　　　　　ADJECTIVE

_____ is _____ .
　　PARTNER 2　　　　　　　　ADJECTIVE

Together they are _____ .
　　　　　　　　　　　ADJECTIVE

All my _____ ,
　　　　　NOUN

_____
　　　　　　　　NAME

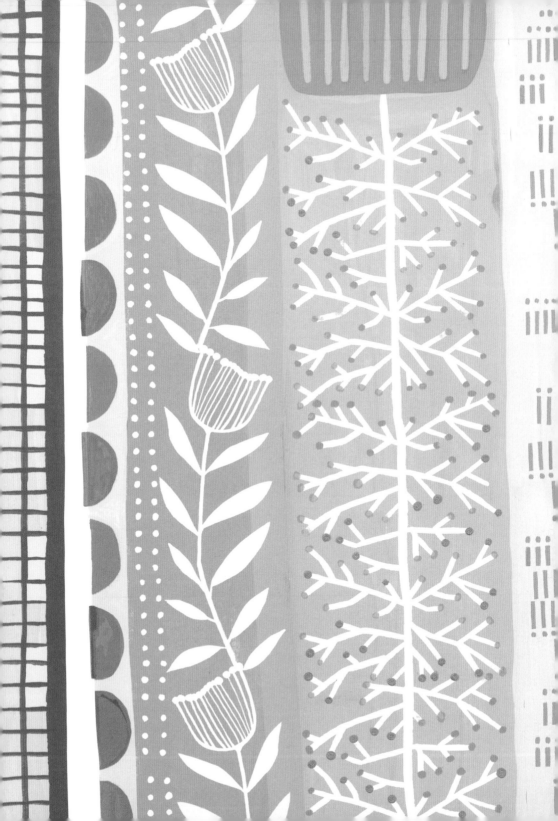

WISHES & ADVICE

The _____ ingredient to a/an _____
        ADJECTIVE   ADJECTIVE

marriage is _____ . In the _____ year,
                  NOUN   LOW NUMBER

you should _____ . In the _____ year,
                                        HIGH NUMBER

you should _____ .

Always _____ . Never _____ .

Occasionally _____ .

You will argue about _____ . It doesn't matter
                          NOUN

because _____ .

My advice in a haiku:

_____
5 SYLLABLES

_____
7 SYLLABLES

_____
5 SYLLABLES

Most of all, I wish you _____ .
                              NOUN

With _____ ,
          NOUN

_____
NAME

ADVENTURES TO SHARE

If the couple was a destination, they would be _____
PLACE

because _____ . On your honeymoon, be sure

to _____ _____ . Don't _____
VERB   NOUN   VERB

_____ . The most _____ trip I've taken was
NOUN   ADJECTIVE

to _____ . The _____ thing I've eaten on
PLACE   ADJECTIVE

vacation was _____ in _____ . One activity
FOOD   PLACE

the couple should try is _____ in _____ .
VERB ENDING IN "ING"   PLACE

A mini-adventure the couple should have together is

_____ .

Top three to-dos for the couple's bucket list:

1. _____   2. _____   3. _____

Draw the couple a picture of your favorite destination:

Wishing you _____ adventures together,
ADJECTIVE

_____
NAME

YOUR STORY

I have known _____ since I was _____ years
PARTNER 1   NUMBER

old. The best way to describe _____ is that they are
PARTNER 1

a/an _____ _____ . My _____
ADJECTIVE   NOUN   ADJECTIVE

memory with _____ happened in _____ .
PARTNER 1   YEAR

We were at _____ with _____ .
PLACE   PERSON/PEOPLE

It was _____ because _____ .
ADJECTIVE

When _____ first introduced me to _____ ,
PARTNER 1   PARTNER 2

I thought, _____ ! My _____
EXCLAMATION   ADJECTIVE

memory of the couple is _____ .

They make the _____ couple because
ADJECTIVE

_____ .

_____ is _____ .
PARTNER 1   ADJECTIVE

_____ is _____ .
PARTNER 2   ADJECTIVE

Together they are _____ .
ADJECTIVE

All my _____ ,
NOUN

_____
NAME

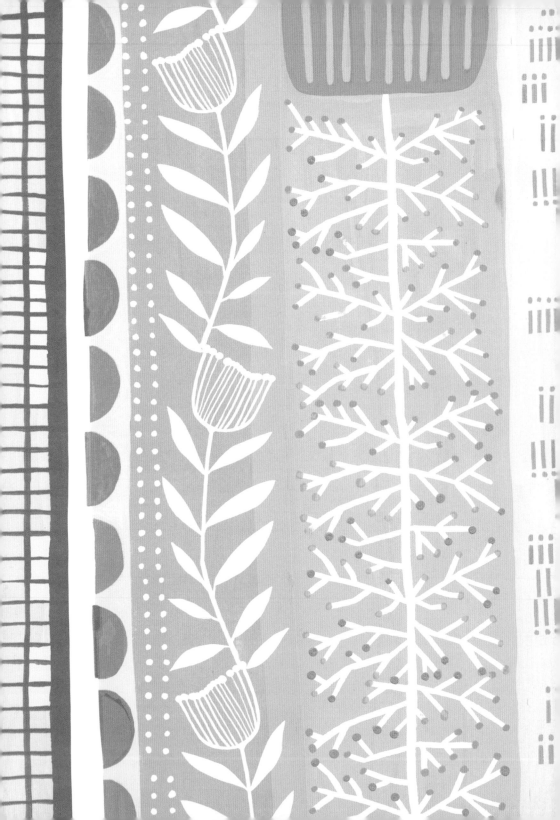

WISHES & ADVICE

The _____ ingredient to a/an _____
         ADJECTIVE   ADJECTIVE

marriage is _____ . In the _____ year,
                    NOUN   LOW NUMBER

you should _____ . In the _____ year,
                                              HIGH NUMBER

you should _____ .

Always _____ . Never _____ .

Occasionally _____ .

You will argue about _____ . It doesn't matter
                              NOUN

because _____ .

My advice in a haiku:

_____
                5 SYLLABLES

_____
                7 SYLLABLES

_____
                5 SYLLABLES

Most of all, I wish you _____ .
                                  NOUN

With _____ ,
              NOUN

_____
                NAME

ADVENTURES TO SHARE

If the couple was a destination, they would be _____
PLACE

because _____ . On your honeymoon, be sure

to _____ _____ . Don't _____
VERB   NOUN   VERB

_____ . The most _____ trip I've taken was
NOUN   ADJECTIVE

to _____ . The _____ thing I've eaten on
PLACE   ADJECTIVE

vacation was _____ in _____ . One activity
FOOD   PLACE

the couple should try is _____ in _____ .
VERB ENDING IN "ING"   PLACE

A mini-adventure the couple should have together is

_____ .

Top three to-dos for the couple's bucket list:

1. _____ 2. _____ 3. _____

Draw the couple a picture of your favorite destination:

Wishing you _____ adventures together,
ADJECTIVE

_____
NAME

YOUR STORY

I have known _____ since I was _____ years
PARTNER 1   NUMBER

old. The best way to describe _____ is that they are
                              PARTNER 1

a/an _____ _____ . My _____
     ADJECTIVE   NOUN   ADJECTIVE

memory with _____ happened in _____ .
            PARTNER 1   YEAR

We were at _____ with _____ .
           PLACE   PERSON/PEOPLE

It was _____ because _____ .
       ADJECTIVE

When _____ first introduced me to _____ ,
     PARTNER 1   PARTNER 2

I thought, _____ ! My _____
           EXCLAMATION   ADJECTIVE

memory of the couple is _____ .

They make the _____ couple because
              ADJECTIVE

_____ .

_____ is _____ .
PARTNER 1   ADJECTIVE

_____ is _____ .
PARTNER 2   ADJECTIVE

Together they are _____ .
                  ADJECTIVE

All my _____ ,
       NOUN

_____
NAME

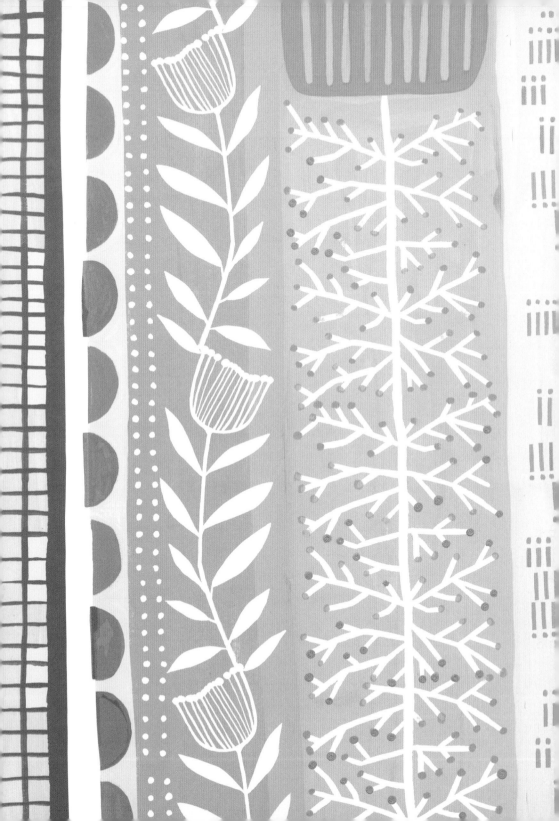

WISHES & ADVICE

The _____ ingredient to a/an _____
      ADJECTIVE   ADJECTIVE

marriage is _____ . In the _____ year,
            NOUN   LOW NUMBER

you should _____ . In the _____ year,
                                HIGH NUMBER

you should _____ .

Always _____ . Never _____ .

Occasionally _____ .

You will argue about _____ . It doesn't matter
                          NOUN

because _____ .

My advice in a haiku:

_____
5 SYLLABLES

_____
7 SYLLABLES

_____
5 SYLLABLES

Most of all, I wish you _____ .
                            NOUN

With _____ ,
       NOUN

_____
NAME

ADVENTURES TO SHARE

If the couple was a destination, they would be _____
                                                          PLACE

because _____ . On your honeymoon, be sure

to _____ _____ . Don't _____
         VERB   NOUN   VERB

_____ . The most _____ trip I've taken was
     NOUN   ADJECTIVE

to _____ . The _____ thing I've eaten on
      PLACE   ADJECTIVE

vacation was _____ in _____ . One activity
                   FOOD   PLACE

the couple should try is _____ in _____ .
                          VERB ENDING IN "ING"   PLACE

A mini-adventure the couple should have together is

_____ .

Top three to-dos for the couple's bucket list:

1. _____ 2. _____ 3. _____

Draw the couple a picture of your favorite destination:

Wishing you _____ adventures together,
                 ADJECTIVE

_____
              NAME

YOUR STORY

I have known _____ since I was _____ years
PARTNER 1   NUMBER

old. The best way to describe _____ is that they are
PARTNER 1

a/an _____ _____ . My _____
ADJECTIVE   NOUN   ADJECTIVE

memory with _____ happened in _____ .
PARTNER 1   YEAR

We were at _____ with _____ .
PLACE   PERSON/PEOPLE

It was _____ because _____ .
ADJECTIVE

When _____ first introduced me to _____ ,
PARTNER 1   PARTNER 2

I thought, _____ ! My _____
EXCLAMATION   ADJECTIVE

memory of the couple is _____ .

They make the _____ couple because
ADJECTIVE

_____ .

_____ is _____ .
PARTNER 1   ADJECTIVE

_____ is _____ .
PARTNER 2   ADJECTIVE

Together they are _____ .
ADJECTIVE

All my _____ ,
NOUN

_____
NAME

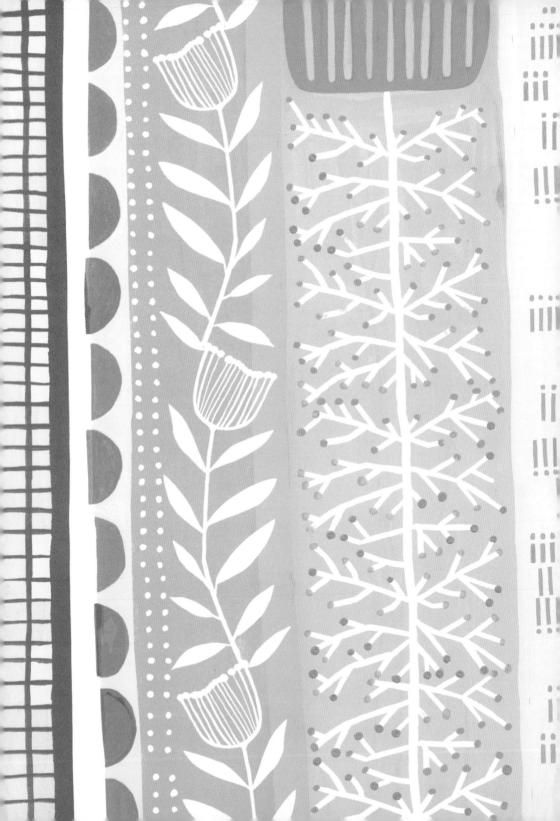

WISHES & ADVICE

The _____ ingredient to a/an _____
     ADJECTIVE   ADJECTIVE

marriage is _____ . In the _____ year,
             NOUN   LOW NUMBER

you should _____ . In the _____ year,
                          HIGH NUMBER

you should _____ .

Always _____ . Never _____ .

Occasionally _____ .

You will argue about _____ . It doesn't matter
                           NOUN

because _____ .

My advice in a haiku:

_____
5 SYLLABLES

_____
7 SYLLABLES

_____
5 SYLLABLES

Most of all, I wish you _____ .
                           NOUN

With _____ ,
          NOUN

_____
NAME

ADVENTURES TO SHARE

If the couple was a destination, they would be _____
PLACE

because _____ . On your honeymoon, be sure

to _____ _____ . Don't _____
VERB   NOUN   VERB

_____ . The most _____ trip I've taken was
NOUN   ADJECTIVE

to _____ . The _____ thing I've eaten on
PLACE   ADJECTIVE

vacation was _____ in _____ . One activity
FOOD   PLACE

the couple should try is _____ in _____ .
VERB ENDING IN "ING"   PLACE

A mini-adventure the couple should have together is

_____ .

Top three to-dos for the couple's bucket list:

1. _____ 2. _____ 3. _____

Draw the couple a picture of your favorite destination:

Wishing you _____ adventures together,
ADJECTIVE

_____
NAME

YOUR STORY

I have known _____ since I was _____ years
PARTNER 1   NUMBER

old. The best way to describe _____ is that they are
PARTNER 1

a/an _____ _____ . My _____
ADJECTIVE   NOUN   ADJECTIVE

memory with _____ happened in _____ .
PARTNER 1   YEAR

We were at _____ with _____ .
PLACE   PERSON/PEOPLE

It was _____ because _____ .
ADJECTIVE

When _____ first introduced me to _____ ,
PARTNER 1   PARTNER 2

I thought, _____ ! My _____
EXCLAMATION   ADJECTIVE

memory of the couple is _____ .

They make the _____ couple because
ADJECTIVE

_____ .

_____ is _____ .
PARTNER 1   ADJECTIVE

_____ is _____ .
PARTNER 2   ADJECTIVE

Together they are _____ .
ADJECTIVE

All my _____ ,
NOUN

_____
NAME

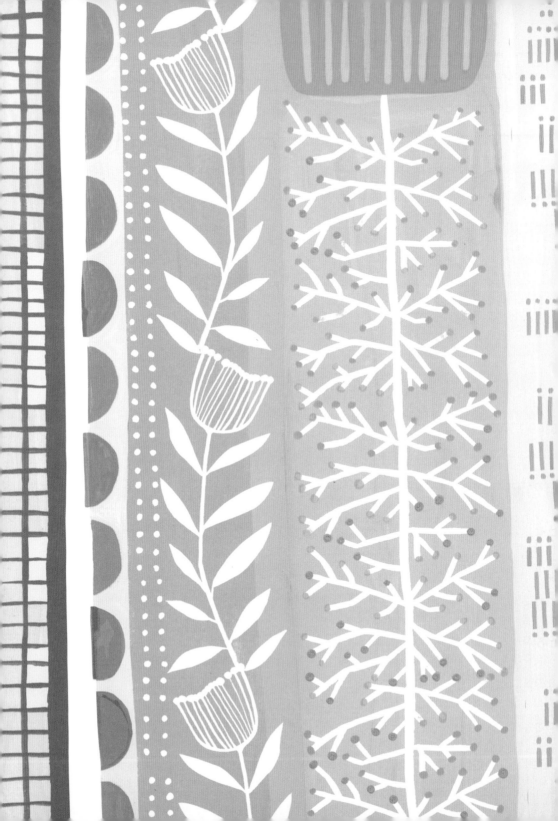

WISHES & ADVICE

The _____ ingredient to a/an _____
     ADJECTIVE   ADJECTIVE

marriage is _____ . In the _____ year,
     NOUN   LOW NUMBER

you should _____ . In the _____ year,
                HIGH NUMBER

you should _____ .

Always _____ . Never _____ .

Occasionally _____ .

You will argue about _____ . It doesn't matter
            NOUN

because _____ .

My advice in a haiku:

_____
5 SYLLABLES

_____
7 SYLLABLES

_____
5 SYLLABLES

Most of all, I wish you _____ .
           NOUN

With _____ ,
     NOUN

_____
NAME

ADVENTURES TO SHARE

If the couple was a destination, they would be _____
PLACE

because _____ . On your honeymoon, be sure

to _____ _____ . Don't _____
VERB   NOUN   VERB

_____ . The most _____ trip I've taken was
NOUN   ADJECTIVE

to _____ . The _____ thing I've eaten on
PLACE   ADJECTIVE

vacation was _____ in _____ . One activity
FOOD   PLACE

the couple should try is _____ in _____ .
VERB ENDING IN "ING"   PLACE

A mini-adventure the couple should have together is

_____ .

Top three to-dos for the couple's bucket list:

1. _____ 2. _____ 3. _____

Draw the couple a picture of your favorite destination:

Wishing you _____ adventures together,
ADJECTIVE

_____
NAME

YOUR STORY

I have known _____ since I was _____ years
                    PARTNER 1   NUMBER

old. The best way to describe _____ is that they are
                                    PARTNER 1

a/an _____ _____ . My _____
         ADJECTIVE   NOUN   ADJECTIVE

memory with _____ happened in _____ .
                  PARTNER 1   YEAR

We were at _____ with _____ .
                  PLACE   PERSON/PEOPLE

It was _____ because _____ .
          ADJECTIVE

When _____ first introduced me to _____ ,
          PARTNER 1   PARTNER 2

I thought, _____ ! My _____
              EXCLAMATION   ADJECTIVE

memory of the couple is _____ .

They make the _____ couple because
                    ADJECTIVE

_____ .

_____ is _____ .
    PARTNER 1   ADJECTIVE

_____ is _____ .
    PARTNER 2   ADJECTIVE

Together they are _____ .
                          ADJECTIVE

All my _____ ,
              NOUN

_____
       NAME

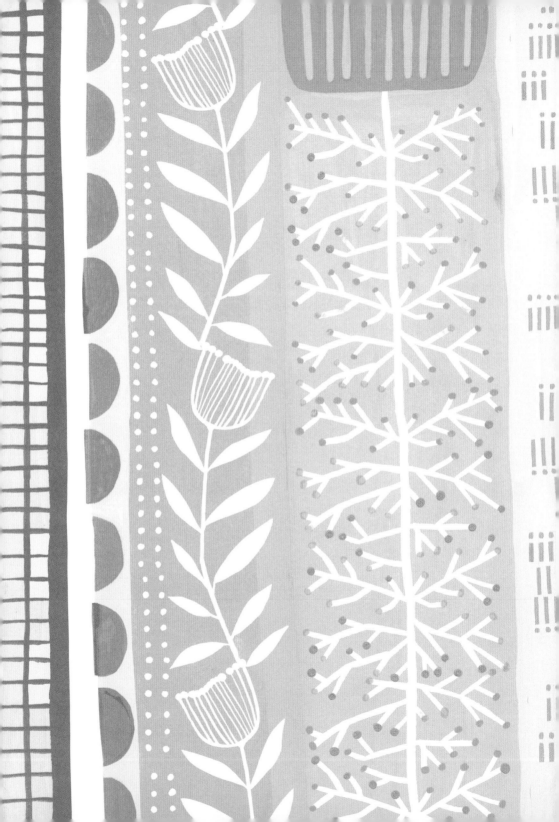

WISHES & ADVICE

The _____ ingredient to a/an _____
       ADJECTIVE   ADJECTIVE

marriage is _____ . In the _____ year,
                  NOUN   LOW NUMBER

you should _____ . In the _____ year,
                                        HIGH NUMBER

you should _____ .

Always _____ . Never _____ .

Occasionally _____ .

You will argue about _____ . It doesn't matter
                            NOUN

because _____ .

My advice in a haiku:

_____
5 SYLLABLES

_____
7 SYLLABLES

_____
5 SYLLABLES

Most of all, I wish you _____ .
                              NOUN

With _____ ,
         NOUN

_____
NAME

ADVENTURES TO SHARE

If the couple was a destination, they would be _____
PLACE

because _____ . On your honeymoon, be sure

to _____ _____ . Don't _____
    VERB   NOUN   VERB

_____ . The most _____ trip I've taken was
   NOUN   ADJECTIVE

to _____ . The _____ thing I've eaten on
   PLACE   ADJECTIVE

vacation was _____ in _____ . One activity
          FOOD   PLACE

the couple should try is _____ in _____ .
          VERB ENDING IN "ING"   PLACE

A mini-adventure the couple should have together is

_____ .

Top three to-dos for the couple's bucket list:

1. _____ 2. _____ 3. _____

Draw the couple a picture of your favorite destination:

Wishing you _____ adventures together,
          ADJECTIVE

_____
NAME

YOUR STORY

I have known _____ since I was _____ years
PARTNER 1   NUMBER

old. The best way to describe _____ is that they are
PARTNER 1

a/an _____ _____ . My _____
ADJECTIVE   NOUN   ADJECTIVE

memory with _____ happened in _____ .
PARTNER 1   YEAR

We were at _____ with _____ .
PLACE   PERSON/PEOPLE

It was _____ because _____ .
ADJECTIVE

When _____ first introduced me to _____ ,
PARTNER 1   PARTNER 2

I thought, _____ ! My _____
EXCLAMATION   ADJECTIVE

memory of the couple is _____ .

They make the _____ couple because
ADJECTIVE

_____ .

_____ is _____ .
PARTNER 1   ADJECTIVE

_____ is _____ .
PARTNER 2   ADJECTIVE

Together they are _____ .
ADJECTIVE

All my _____ ,
NOUN

_____
NAME

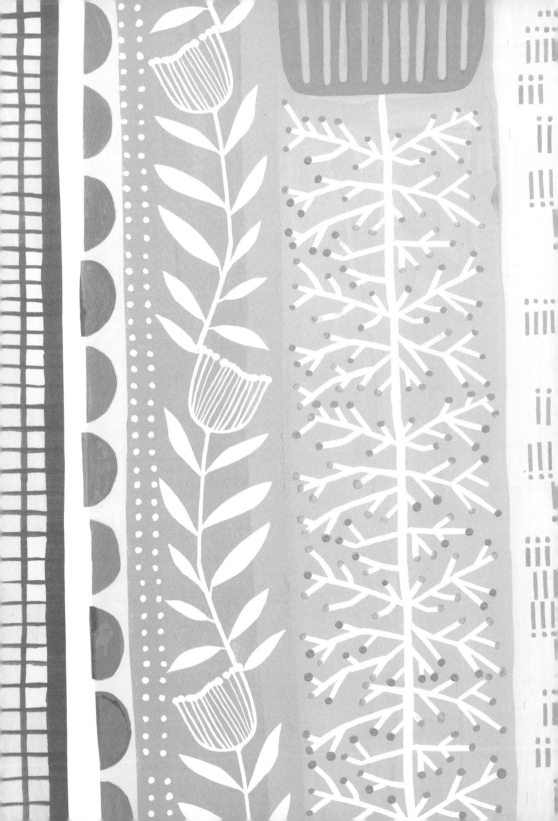

WISHES & ADVICE

The _____ ingredient to a/an _____
      ADJECTIVE   ADJECTIVE

marriage is _____ . In the _____ year,
              NOUN   LOW NUMBER

you should _____ . In the _____ year,
                                  HIGH NUMBER

you should _____ .

Always _____ . Never _____ .

Occasionally _____ .

You will argue about _____ . It doesn't matter
                        NOUN

because _____ .

My advice in a haiku:

_____
5 SYLLABLES

_____
7 SYLLABLES

_____
5 SYLLABLES

Most of all, I wish you _____ .
                            NOUN

With _____ ,
        NOUN

_____
NAME

ADVENTURES TO SHARE

If the couple was a destination, they would be _____
PLACE

because _____ . On your honeymoon, be sure

to _____ _____ . Don't _____
VERB   NOUN   VERB

_____ . The most _____ trip I've taken was
NOUN   ADJECTIVE

to _____ . The _____ thing I've eaten on
PLACE   ADJECTIVE

vacation was _____ in _____ . One activity
FOOD   PLACE

the couple should try is _____ in _____ .
VERB ENDING IN "ING"   PLACE

A mini-adventure the couple should have together is

_____ .

Top three to-dos for the couple's bucket list:

1. _____ 2. _____ 3. _____

Draw the couple a picture of your favorite destination:

Wishing you _____ adventures together,
ADJECTIVE

_____
NAME

YOUR STORY

I have known _____ since I was _____ years
PARTNER 1   NUMBER

old. The best way to describe _____ is that they are
PARTNER 1

a/an _____ _____ . My _____
ADJECTIVE   NOUN   ADJECTIVE

memory with _____ happened in _____ .
PARTNER 1   YEAR

We were at _____ with _____ .
PLACE   PERSON/PEOPLE

It was _____ because _____ .
ADJECTIVE

When _____ first introduced me to _____ ,
PARTNER 1   PARTNER 2

I thought, _____ ! My _____
EXCLAMATION   ADJECTIVE

memory of the couple is _____ .

They make the _____ couple because
ADJECTIVE

_____ .

_____ is _____ .
PARTNER 1   ADJECTIVE

_____ is _____ .
PARTNER 2   ADJECTIVE

Together they are _____ .
ADJECTIVE

All my _____ ,
NOUN

_____
NAME

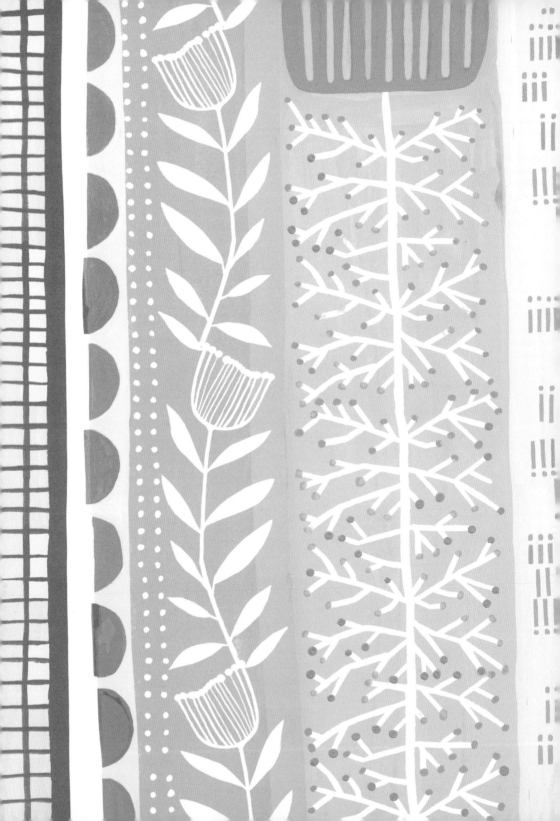

WISHES & ADVICE

The _____ ingredient to a/an _____
           ADJECTIVE   ADJECTIVE

marriage is _____ . In the _____ year,
                    NOUN   LOW NUMBER

you should _____ . In the _____ year,
                                          HIGH NUMBER

you should _____ .

Always _____ . Never _____ .

Occasionally _____ .

You will argue about _____ . It doesn't matter
                              NOUN

because _____ .

My advice in a haiku:

_____
              5 SYLLABLES

_____
              7 SYLLABLES

_____
              5 SYLLABLES

Most of all, I wish you _____ .
                                NOUN

With _____ ,
            NOUN

_____
              NAME

ADVENTURES TO SHARE

If the couple was a destination, they would be _____
PLACE

because _____ . On your honeymoon, be sure

to _____ _____ . Don't _____
VERB   NOUN   VERB

_____ . The most _____ trip I've taken was
NOUN   ADJECTIVE

to _____ . The _____ thing I've eaten on
PLACE   ADJECTIVE

vacation was _____ in _____ . One activity
FOOD   PLACE

the couple should try is _____ in _____ .
VERB ENDING IN "ING"   PLACE

A mini-adventure the couple should have together is

_____ .

Top three to-dos for the couple's bucket list:

1. _____ 2. _____ 3. _____

Draw the couple a picture of your favorite destination:

Wishing you _____ adventures together,
ADJECTIVE

_____
NAME

YOUR STORY

I have known _____ since I was _____ years
                PARTNER 1   NUMBER

old. The best way to describe _____ is that they are
                                  PARTNER 1

a/an _____ _____ . My _____
       ADJECTIVE   NOUN   ADJECTIVE

memory with _____ happened in _____ .
                PARTNER 1   YEAR

We were at _____ with _____ .
                PLACE   PERSON/PEOPLE

It was _____ because _____ .
          ADJECTIVE

When _____ first introduced me to _____ ,
         PARTNER 1   PARTNER 2

I thought, _____ ! My _____
              EXCLAMATION   ADJECTIVE

memory of the couple is _____ .

They make the _____ couple because
                   ADJECTIVE

_____ .

_____ is _____ .
    PARTNER 1   ADJECTIVE

_____ is _____ .
    PARTNER 2   ADJECTIVE

Together they are _____ .
                       ADJECTIVE

All my _____ ,
           NOUN

_____
      NAME

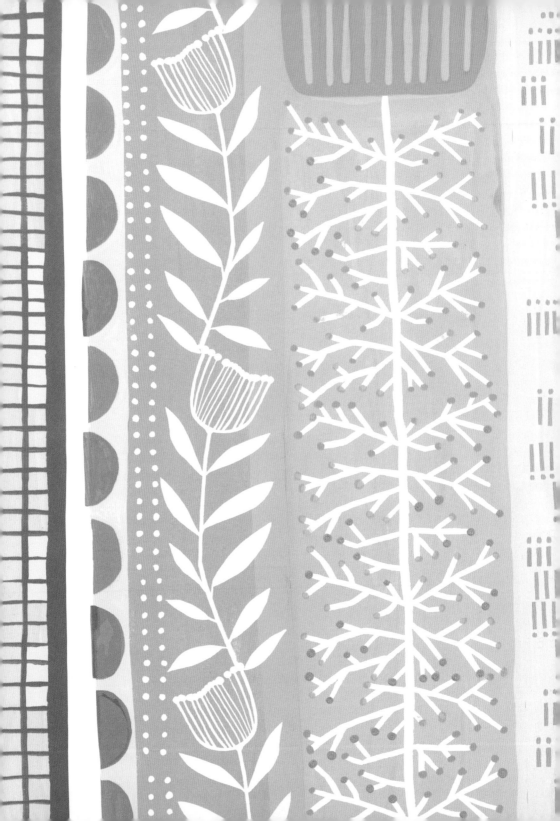

WISHES & ADVICE

The _____ ingredient to a/an _____
      ADJECTIVE   ADJECTIVE

marriage is _____ . In the _____ year,
                    NOUN   LOW NUMBER

you should _____ . In the _____ year,
                                              HIGH NUMBER

you should _____ .

Always _____ . Never _____ .

Occasionally _____ .

You will argue about _____ . It doesn't matter
                              NOUN

because _____ .

My advice in a haiku:

_____
             5 SYLLABLES

_____
             7 SYLLABLES

_____
             5 SYLLABLES

Most of all, I wish you _____ .
                                    NOUN

With _____ ,
              NOUN

_____
             NAME

ADVENTURES TO SHARE

If the couple was a destination, they would be _____
                                                    PLACE

because _____ . On your honeymoon, be sure

to _____ _____ . Don't _____
       VERB   NOUN   VERB

_____ . The most _____ trip I've taken was
       NOUN   ADJECTIVE

to _____ . The _____ thing I've eaten on
        PLACE   ADJECTIVE

vacation was _____ in _____ . One activity
                    FOOD   PLACE

the couple should try is _____ in _____ .
                          VERB ENDING IN "ING"   PLACE

A mini-adventure the couple should have together is

_____ .

Top three to-dos for the couple's bucket list:

1. _____   2. _____   3. _____

Draw the couple a picture of your favorite destination:

Wishing you _____ adventures together,
                  ADJECTIVE

_____
                NAME